PEPPER and PARSLEY

IN the KItcheN

Written and Illustrated by
the Stone and Theris families

First Edition, 2019

ISBN: 978-1-7923-0648-8

Mint Leaf Media
Mintleafmedia.com

Published by Mint Leaf Media

INDEX

DEDICATED TO

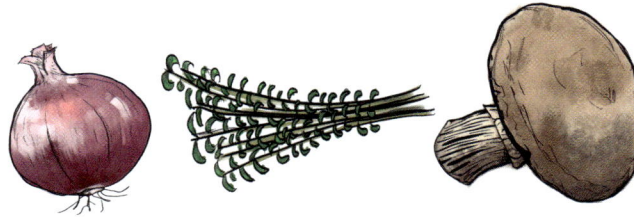

"My Yiaya, who taught me how to explore my first kitchen."
-Alexandra

"My mother, Joanne, who taught me that educating children is the most rewarding gift in life."
-Nathaniel

"My broccoli-loving, kombucha-drinking, sushi-eating ice cream monsters, Pepper and Parsley. The best tiny humans I know."
-Elizabeth & Spike

Pepper and Parsley, what will the day bring?
Let's walk through the garden! Let's hear the birds sing.

Oh look! How they've sprouted!
Oh look! How they've grown!

From the Earth came these gifts where the seeds were once sown.

We'll take two heads of corn,

and mushrooms if you please.

Potatoes, carrots and onions, plus the garlic and sweet peas!

Let's plan a great meal and our work will transcend
As we prepare for the gift of time spent with a friend!

We are so excited to see our friend "Danil".
He has come to visit us from the land of Brazil.

"Will you help us, Danil, and share a family tradition?"

We found food in our garden to cook in the kitchen!

Look out! Be alert. You are in a new place.
Let's explore our environment to learn what is safe.

Hold the vegetables in place and tuck your fingers away.
Be aware of the heat and safe we will stay.

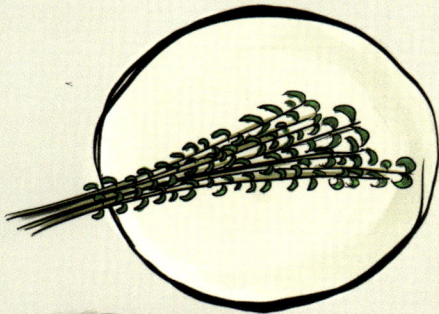

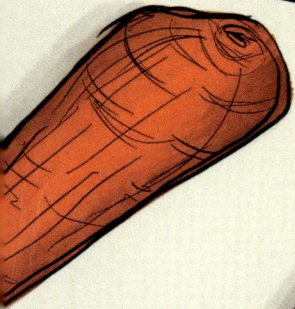

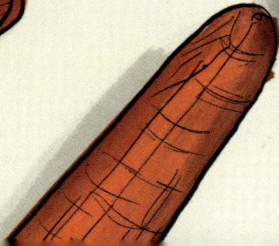

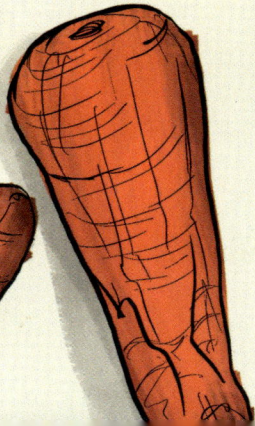

These roots are delicious! Let's give them a try.
We'll mix herbs from our garden and bake a pot pie!

First we chop veggies, then slowly mix in a roux.
Once the crust is rolled out, we know what to do!

We'll top off our crust with this savory filling.
Let's cover it with dough and be mindful of spilling!

Into the oven! Mom's help we will need!
Let's cook this pie safely and our family we'll feed.

Our meal has created a bond no one would expect.

Let's share our adventure and see what will come next!

Pepper smiled as she thought, "What a wonderful treat!
So many dishes to cook! SO many people to meet!"

RESOURCE SECTION

At Pepper and Parsley, we believe that education starts at birth. With this in mind, we have constructed this resource section to help you guide infants, toddlers, preschoolers and elementary school children in home kitchens around the world. Cooking with young children is a great way to include your entire family in daily routines and is an excellent way to foster independence, concentration, coordination and self-confidence in your children. In this section, you will find a map and a dual language glossary featuring illustrations and vocabulary terms in both English and Portuguese. You will also find a visual recipe designed to develop your children's strengths in following directions and identifying patterns as well as in a variety of mathematical concepts. The glossary and visual recipe help your child learn independent cooking skills. With your help, they can create a vegetable pot pie for your family to enjoy. This resource section also contains two Montessori-inspired lessons and guides for parents. The first is an introductory lesson to chopping vegetables. The second is a guide for a pie preparation. These lessons are intended for parents to practice and prepare in order to guide their children through the book's visual recipe. We have included a few helpful tips for presenting lessons to small children below:

- Prepare a workspace in your kitchen that is easily accessible for your child to reach with both feet on the floor.

- Be sure to prep the ingredients before introducing the lesson to your child (vegetables are easily chopped after cutting into small thin sections that lay flat against the cutting board. Ingredients are easily measured after placing in containers intended for small hands).

- Young children learn by observing. Remember to move and to speak slowly when demonstrating a lesson.

After a decade of cooking with small children both in the classroom and at home, we have learned a lot about what works and even more about how to overcome challenges. Preparing a kitchen environment for a child's independence and success is what we do best! We are excited to share this resource section with your family and hope that the tools in the following pages guide your cooking together at home. May Pepper and Parsley inspire both you and your children in this kitchen adventure and many more!

With joy,

Your friends at Pepper and Parsley

INGREDIENTS

Carrot
Cenoura

Onion
Cebola

Peas
Ervilhas

Potato
Batata

Celery
Aipo

Corn
Milho

Mushrooms
Cogumelo

Cream
Creme

Salt
Sal

Pepper
Pimenta

Garlic
Alho

Parsley
Salsinha

Thyme
Tomilho

Eggs
Ovos

Butter
Manteiga

Flour
Farinha

Pastry dough
Massa folhada

TOOLS

Whisk
Batedor

Spatula
Espátula

Rolling pin
Rola de massa

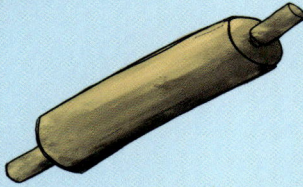

Pie tin
Forma de torta

Pastry brush
Escova de pastelaria

Knife
Faca

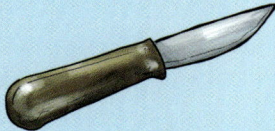

Vegetable chopper
Cortador de legumes

Vegetable peeler
Descascador de legumes

Garlic press
Espremedor de alho

Cutting board
Tábua de cortar

Kitchen scissors
Tesoura de cozinha

Fork
Garfo

Oven mitt
Luva de forno

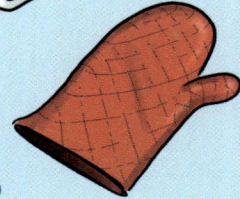

Help
Ajuda

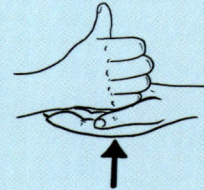

Please
Por favor

VISUAL RECIPE

 +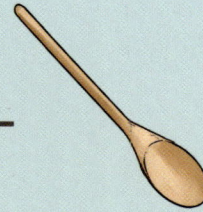

Mix the following together

2 carrots (chopped) 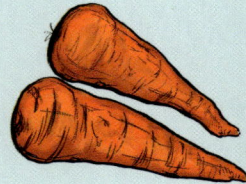 +  +

1 onion (chopped)  +  +

3 branches celery stalk (chopped)  +  +

1 potato (chopped)  +  +

8oz mushrooms (sliced)  +  +

2 cups peas (frozen or fresh)  +

1 cup corn (frozen or fresh)  +

4 cloves garlic (minced)  +

2 tbsp fresh thyme (chopped)  +  +

1/2 cup fresh parsley (chopped)  +  +

3 tsp salt  +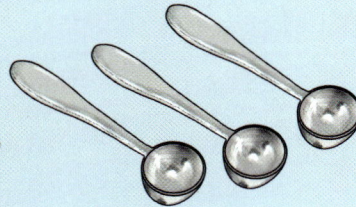

2 tsp pepper  +

MAKE THE ROUX

3 tbsp butter (melt)

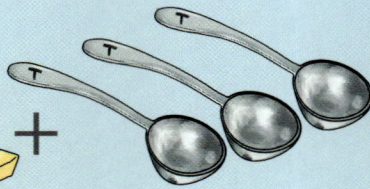

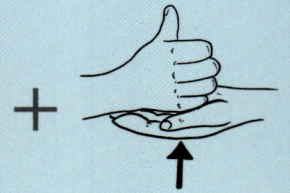

1/2cup all purpose flour

MAKE THE SAUCE

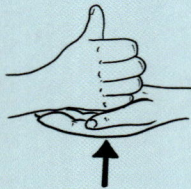

4 cups vegetable stock
(thickened w/ roux)

1 cups heavy cream

Blend seasoned vegetables and sauce together

PiE PREPARATION

*Follow our pie preparation lesson for a step by step guide

Prepare pie tin

Fill the pie

Cover the pie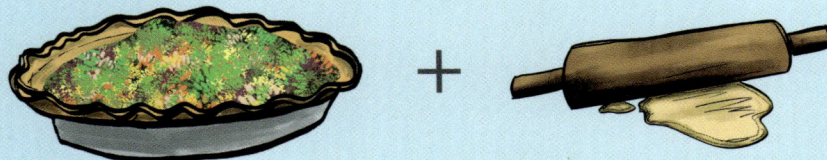

Vent the pie

Finish with an egg wash

Bake the pie

28

VEGETABLE CHOPPING

Materials:
- Clean vegetables in a basket
- Small cutting board
- Paring knife or Montessori wavy chopper
- Small bowl for prepped vegetables

Presentation:

1. Say, "I will show you how to chop a/an (carrot, onion, mushroom, celery)".
2. Walk to the sink and wash your hands.
3. Walk to the food prep area.
4. With two hands, place the cutting board in the center of the prep area.
5. Hold the vegetable stationary with the left hand (tucking your fingers and thumb).
6. Carefully pick up the chopping tool (or paring knife) with the right hand.
7. Cut off the ends of the vegetable. Place the cutting tool gently on the table. Throw ends in the wastebasket or compost.
8. Grasp the vegetable with the left hand (fingers and thumb tucked).
9. Carefully grasp the cutting tool with the right hand.
10. Chop or slice the vegetable slowly moving the left hand (fingers/thumb tucked) down the vegetable slowly to stabilize while moving the right hand away from the left.
11. Place the pieces/slices into a small bowl to the right of the cutting board.
12. Replace the tools to their original position.
13. Say, "I chopped/sliced the.....(vegetable)".

*Tip for parents: Prep the vegetables first by cutting them in half horizontally so that the vegetable sits flat on the cutting board for your child.

PIE PREPARATION

Materials:
- 1 tbsp flour
- 1 tbsp butter
- 2 (2)inch sections of dough rolled into spheres
- 1/2 tbsp (measuring spoon)
- Mini pie tin
- Child sized rolling pin
- Small fork
- Tray

Presentation:

1. Say, "I will show you how to prepare the pie".
2. Walk to the sink and wash your hands.
3. Walk to the food prep area.
4. Grab the butter with the left hand and gently peel the paper away then return to it's original position.
5. Hold the pie tin in the left hand and spread the butter in a circular motion with the right hand.
6. Walk to the sink and wash your hands.
7. Walk to the food prep area.
8. Measure 1/2 tablespoon of flour and transfer it into the pie tin.
9. Gently shake the pie tin in a circular motion to spread the flour evenly in the pan.
10. Say, "The pie tin is prepared for dough".
11. Measure 1/2 tablespoon flour and gently shake it over the work area.
12. Remove 1 section of dough and press into the floured area.
13. Lift dough with left hand and flip into the flour.
14. Grab the rolling pin with two hands and hold over the dough.
15. Say, "Press firmly, then roll".
16. With two hands press and roll the dough vertically (repeat horizontally).
17. When the dough is rolled thin say, "I rolled the dough".
18. Place rolling pin at the top of dough and gently roll onto the pin.
19. Hold the pie tin with the right hand and gently unroll the dough into the tin.
20. Using the pads of fingers from both hands gently press the dough into the pan.
21. Say, "The pie is ready to fill".
    *After filling the pie repeat the dough rolling process with the second section and cover the pie.
22. Hold the pie tin with the left hand and gently fold the excess dough around the pie tin in a circular motion with the right hand.
23. Grab the fork with the right hand and repeat the circular motion by gently pressing the fork around the edge of the pie.
24. Lift the fork over the center of the pie and say, "The pie needs a vent".
    Gently prick the pie with a fork three times around the center.
25. Say, "It's time to bake the pie".
    *Author's note: This method can be used for any type of pie; simply add fresh fruit, honey, and cinnamon for a delicious desert twist on our favorite pie preparation lesson.
    **Optional: Crack and beat an egg then brush the top of the pie with a pastry brush for an added sheen.

VEGETABLE POT PIE (FULL RECIPE)

Filling:

2 carrots (chopped)
1 onion (chopped)
3 branches celery stalk (chopped)
1 potato (chopped)
8 oz baby bella mushrooms (sliced)
1 cup corn (frozen or fresh)
2 cups organic peas (frozen or fresh)
4 cloves garlic (minced)
2 tbsp fresh thyme
1/2 cup fresh parsley leaves
2 tsp salt
1 tsp pepper
3 tbsp organic extra virgin olive oil
4 cups vegetable stock
1 cup heavy cream

Roux:

3 tbsp salted butter (melt)
1/2 cup all purpose flour

Pie:

2 rolls pastry dough (1 box prepared)
2 tbsp all purpose flour
2 tbsp butter
2 eggs beaten

33

Method:

Preheat oven to 350 degrees.

Finely chop onion, carrots, celery, and potato then add garlic, corn and peas in a large bowl. Add salt, pepper and freshly chopped parsley and thyme. Mix ingredients with olive oil and set aside.

In a small saucepan bring vegetable stock to a rolling boil. Heat butter and slowly whisk in flour to make a smooth roux. Quickly whisk roux into vegetable stock. After thickening the stock with roux, carefully mix in the seasoned vegetables. Simmer for 10-15 minutes. Once vegetables are tender reduce heat and stir in cream. Remove from heat and let sit to room temperature.

While the sauce cools prepare 4 mini pie tins with butter and flour. Using kitchen scissors cut dough into four equal sections. Roll each section of pastry dough out onto a floured surface. Line each pie tin with a thin layer of dough. Carefully fill each pie with mixture. Using kitchen scissors divide second roll of dough into four equal sections. Roll each section onto a floured surface. Cover each pie with dough. Using kitchen scissors trim any excess dough before carefully folding around the perimeter of each pie. With a small fork, gently press around the edge of the pie to seal before piercing the center of each pie to vent. Beat two eggs and brush each pie before baking for 25-30 minutes or until golden brown. Let cool and enjoy. Serves 4.

About the Authors

Spike Stone is an artist, writer, scientist and adventurer living in Providence, Rhode Island with his intrepid entrepreneur wife Elizabeth Stone and two daughters Pepper and Violet Parsley. Together this is Spike and Elizabeth's third book,one as a publisher and the other as an illustrator. The Stone family enjoys traveling and is always eager to learn and explore the world around them. The Stone family teamed up with the Theris family when Pepper became the first student at Tiger Lily Montessori with Violet Parsley soon to follow.

Nathaniel and Alexandra Theris live in Providence, Rhode Island's "East Side" neighborhood and enjoy creating materials and cooking lessons for students in their small Montessori program, Tiger Lily Montessori School. Nathaniel is a writer and a chef who has lived in fifteen countries around the world. Alexandra is the Founding Head of School and toddler teacher at Tiger Lily Montessori School. She holds an Infant/Toddler (0-3) credential from The American Montessori Society (AMS) and has been working with children for 15 years.